Ella

How a sad girl learns she's perfect just the way she is.

Marisa Chiorello

Illustrations by Michelle Colli

Showtime Books
Staten Island, New York

Published by Showtime Books
140 Sheldon Ave.,
Staten Island, N.Y. 10312
www.showtimepublications.com

© 2017 Marisa Chiorello
Illustrations © 2017 Michelle Colli

All rights reserved. No part of this book may be reproduced in any form or by any electronic or mechanical means, including information storage and retrieval systems, without permission in writing from the publisher, except by a reviewer who may quote brief passages in a review.

ISBN 978-0-9911860-0-6

Story is set in 18 pt. Futura Book
Body text is Minion Pro

For Olivia:
My sister,
my best friend
and my constant inspiration.
I love you with all my heart.

For All the Girls Out There:
You are beautiful just the way you are.
Never, **ever** *doubt it!*

Introduction

When I was young, I realized that I did not look like my friends, or even like other girls in my school. My body shape was different. My tan skin, dark brown eyes and dark hair stood out. Most other girls were thin. They had light skin, pale blue eyes and blonde hair. They were beautiful Barbie dolls. Miniature Britney Spears, Christina Aguileras and Baby Spices. I was the odd girl out. The ugly duckling. Or so I thought.

Oh, how I wished I could have looked *exactly* like they looked! In my mind, those qualities made them beautiful. Or so I thought.

There was nothing, or no one, to tell me I was wrong.

The desire to alter my physical appearance grew stronger as I entered high school. Now, fashion magazines, such as *Seventeen* and *Teen Vogue*, played a role, too. Page by page, I immersed myself in the images of fashion models and actresses. They all sported blonde hair, light skin, slender waists, protruding bones and flat stomachs. These images became etched in my mind. This to me was the epitome of beauty. To be beautiful I'd have to change my physical appearance. Or so I thought.

The transformation began innocently enough. I began daily exercise. Then I ate less food. Sure enough, the extra weight began to disappear. Before long I was spiraling out of control. I became obsessed with exercising. I feared food. I was paranoid of gaining weight. One day I looked in a mirror. I saw my bones protruding, just like the models in the fashion magazines.

Ideal beauty! I've made it! Or so I thought.

In my quest to become beautiful, however, I soon realized I had lost something quite valuable. I had lost myself. Over-exercising, fear of eating and the paranoia of weight gain was certainly no way to live.

In college, I decided to major in Women's and Gender Studies. Early on, I enrolled in a Gender Studies class. It was in that class that I learned all about girls and body image. I read *Future Girl: Young Women in the Twenty-First Century*, by Anita Harris. Harris writes about the "can-do" girl, the fashion magazine model to whom girls are exposed. We are "taught" that we must have this specific appearance to be the "can-do" girl. She is beauty. She is success. If we don't look *exactly* like her, we are failures. Or so I thought.

I also read *Enlightened Sexism: The Seductive Message that Feminisim's Work is Done,* by Susan J. Douglass. Here I discovered the correlation between eating disorders and magazines. Many magazines show images of "hyperthin" beautiful women. Girls regularly read these magazines — then become critical and unhappy with their bodies, Douglass writes. They see themselves as fat and ugly because they don't mirror female images in fashion magazines. So they begin self-starvation or binging and purging. They hope to mold themselves into that ideal image. *They want to be beautiful — so they need to be thin.* Or so they think.

Here's the scary truth: girls today as young as five and six years old are developing eating disorders and reporting body dissatisfaction. Think about it. *Five and six years old!*

Through the story of young Ella, my message to girls is simple: they don't need to look like anyone else. They are beautiful just the way they are!

I dedicate this book to young women and their parents everywhere. I certainly hope Ella's story will truly inspire and educate.

— *Marisa Chiorello*

Ella is a happy little girl.

She likes to dance.

She likes to sing.

She likes to give big hugs.

She's always laughing.

She's always smiling.

She's always happy.

Even on rainy days.

Her family calls her their little ray of sunshine.

But one day, Ella began to change.

She happened to find her big sister's fashion magazines.

So she sat down to look at the pictures.

Ella noticed something odd.

All the girls looked different than she looked.

Much, much different.

They had straight blonde hair. Ella didn't.

They had blue eyes. Ella didn't.

They had fair skin. Ella didn't.

They even had tiny tummies. Ella didn't.

Ella began to wonder, "Where are the girls who look like I do?"

She turned each page, looking for girls with rings of bouncy, round curls.

She searched for girls with green eyes… with tan skin…and with bigger tummies than she had.

Sadly, she found none.

Ella looked at herself.

And a tear slowly rolled down her cheek.

As days passed, Ella wasn't a happy little girl anymore.

She didn't dance.

She didn't sing.

She didn't smile.

She didn't even give big hugs.

Ella was very, very sad.

She was not a ray of sunshine anymore.

So, one day, Ella looked in a mirror.

She looked. And she looked. And she looked.

She didn't like what she saw.

"I'm an ugly duckling," Ella said.

Then she got an idea.

"I'll change the way I look," she said. "Then I'll look just like those girls in the magazines!"

First, Ella brushed out each bouncy curl.

This made her hair nice and puffy.

Like a rabbit's fur.

"Can I straighten my hair like you do every morning?" Ella asked her sister.

"Sure," her sister answered.

Pretty soon, Ella's hair was perfectly straight. Exactly like those girls in the magazines!

Ella knew she couldn't change the color of her eyes.

And she couldn't change the color of her skin.

But she really dreamed of a tiny tummy.

"The pretty girls in the magazines don't have all this," she thought as she raised her shirt and poked at her big tummy.

Then Ella got another idea.

She ran to the kitchen.

She threw out the ice cream.

She threw out the potato chips.

She threw out the stacks of cookies in the cookie jar.

Ella even stopped eating.

"Good," she told herself. "Now I'll have a tiny tummy!"

Before long, Ella's sister realized that Ella looked different.

"Why are you trying to look different?" her sister asked.

"Because I don't look like the girls in your magazines," Ella answered. "That's why."

"They're pretty. I'm not."

And then Ella began to cry.

Ella's sister put her arm around her.

And they held each other real tight.

"You're right, Ella. You're . . . not. . . . pretty," her sister said slowly.

"You're beautiful," she yelled.

"Watch," she said to Ella.

She picked up the mirror.

"See these curls? her sister said. "They're just as bouncy as when you dance and laugh.

"See your tan skin?" her sister continued. "It's as beautiful as golden honey.

"And see your tummy?" she said with a tickle. "Well ...

… that tummy of yours is home to pokes … to tickles … to belly raspberries … even to delicious ice cream. It's perfect."

Then Ella's sister hugged her.

"You don't have to look like those girls in my fashion magazines, Ella.

"You're perfect just the way you are.

"You are beautiful just by being you."

Ella gave her sister a big, big hug.

And a big, big smile.

She finally realized that each of her qualities is what makes her special.

Ella knows now that she never has to change.

She is a beautiful little girl *just the way she is!*

Acknowledgments

First and foremost, I would like to thank my family for supporting me, for helping me remain confident, and for filling my life with unconditional love. Special thanks to my Dad for giving me strength and encouragement to write this book. Thank you to my younger sister, Olivia, for reviewing my draft manuscript. You believed in me from the beginning, and you continue to be my inspiration. Thank you to my cousin, Hannah Slimak, the inspiration behind Ella's personality, her beautiful curly hair and her awesome fashion sense. You are the fiercest girl I know! Thank you to Bob Williams of Showtime Books. You had faith in the words I wrote — and you had faith in the important message Ella sends to every girl. Without you, this book wouldn't have been published. And readers certainly couldn't have seen Ella if it wasn't for the artistic skill of illustrator Michelle Colli. You brought Ella to life, Michelle, through your special creativity and wonderful talent. Thank you.

About the Author

Growing up, Marisa Chiorello says she always had a passion for writing — and a strong desire to help others. Marisa earned her bachelor's degree from the College of New Jersey, majoring in English Literature and Women's and Gender Studies. It was during her undergraduate years that her love of writing, feminism and helping young women blossomed. So she decided to enter the world of children's books. Marisa says her writing is designed to address topics that she feels must be discussed today. Through her work, she hopes to inspire, encourage, educate and provide confidence to children everywhere. Marisa lives in Hamilton, N.J.

About the Illustrator

Michelle Colli is a self-taught artist who has been illustrating from an early age. She says she loves to introduce colors and expressions into her work. As an art instructor, Michelle says, her creativity comes out and her fun personality shines.

www.ingramcontent.com/pod-product-compliance
Lightning Source LLC
Chambersburg PA
CBHW042059290426
44113CB00001B/17